Original title:
Winter's Silence

Copyright © 2024 Swan Charm
All rights reserved.

Author: Mirell Mesipuu
ISBN HARDBACK: 978-9916-79-978-9
ISBN PAPERBACK: 978-9916-79-979-6
ISBN EBOOK: 978-9916-79-980-2

Secrets Beneath the Snow

Whispers hidden in the white,
Silent tales of winter's night.
Footprints vanish, dreams delayed,
Secrets bloom, though they are frayed.

Gentle flakes, a delicate shroud,
Nature's hush, a tender crowd.
Beneath the frost, life waits anew,
In the stillness, hope breaks through.

Buds nestle close, sleeping deep,
In silence, they begin to creep.
Winter's heart, a quiet gate,
Guarding stories, love and fate.

As the sun starts to rise high,
Melting magic, soft as sigh.
Revealing paths that once were lost,
In every flake, there lies the frost.

Secrets whispered with each breeze,
Nature's secrets carried with ease.
In the thaw, we find the glow,
Of all the wonders beneath the snow.

Tranquil Embrace of Chill

In the grasp of winter's breath,
Every moment holds its depth.
A quiet calm, the world unwinds,
In chilled air, solace finds.

Branches bare, yet strong they stand,
Embraced gently by nature's hand.
In the twilight, shadows play,
Whispers dance at the close of day.

Moonlit nights, a silver sheen,
Calm reflections, peaceful scene.
Frosted edges, dreams unfold,
In the stillness, stories told.

The rhythm slows, the heartbeats hush,
In this quiet, all things rush.
Yet here within this frozen bliss,
We find the warmth in nature's kiss.

Tranquil moments, sweet and still,
Breath of winter, gentle thrill.
In the silence, life remains,
Carried softly through winter's veins.

Echoing Silence of Frosted Nights

Stars like diamonds light the sky,
In the hush, we hear the sigh.
Frosted whispers fill the air,
A world asleep, beyond compare.

Silent shadows weave and sway,
Guided by the moon's soft ray.
Blankets thick upon the ground,
In this peace, dreams are found.

Crystals sparkle, nature's art,
Every glimmer plays its part.
In the stillness, secrets dwell,
Echoes of our hearts that swell.

As we wander, steps are light,
In the echo of frosted night.
Every breath a silent song,
Merging with the night so long.

Echoes linger, soft and sweet,
Carried gently on the street.
In the silence, love is near,
Frosted nights, forever dear.

A Crescendo of Softness

Winter comes with a tender touch,
Every flake, a softened hush.
Nature sings in quiet tones,
In every drift, a heart atones.

Melodies of the chilled air rise,
Wrapped in layers, gentle ties.
Snowflakes fall, a blanket wide,
In this softness, feelings bide.

A symphony of silence plays,
In the night, the world obeys.
With every breath, a soft refrain,
A crescendo of calm, no pain.

Footsteps echo, hush, and glide,
In the frosty dream, we bide.
Whispers curl in the crisp night still,
In the softness, spirits fill.

A crescendo grows, fades away,
Leaving echoes of yesterday.
Winter's grace, a tender muse,
In every snowflake, love we choose.

Shadows on White

In the morning light's embrace,
Shadows dance with whispered grace.
Footprints linger, tales untold,
On the canvas pure and cold.

Branches shiver, silhouettes play,
Softly edging into the day.
Sky above, a pale blue sea,
Cradles dreams of what might be.

Shifting shapes in silence flow,
Like the secrets we don't know.
Fleeting moments, time withstands,
Etching wonders in the sands.

Every shadow, a fleeting spark,
Leads us gently through the dark.
A world woven with soft light,
In the dance of shadowed sight.

A Frozen Interlude

Crystal branches reach for skies,
Silent whispers, nature lies.
Every breath a misty breath,
In this pause, a dream of death.

Snowflakes fall like whispered sighs,
Blanketing the world in guise.
Hushed the ground, a tranquil sheet,
Where time slows, and moments meet.

Stillness wraps the earth so tight,
Embracing all with purest white.
In this frozen, silent space,
Memories melt, then leave no trace.

Nature's art, each flake unique,
In the stillness, hearts can speak.
A frozen interlude, we find,
Piece by piece, our souls unwind.

Still Waters Run Cold

In the twilight's gentle hold,
Still waters run, deep and cold.
Reflections dance upon the face,
Of a world in slow embrace.

Ripples tremble, secrets drown,
Underneath the surface brown.
Beneath the peace, chaos swirls,
Whispered tales of distant worlds.

Dragonflies in fleeting flight,
Swaying softly, catching light.
Time is lost in nature's hymn,
A quiet heart, a world so dim.

Each moment slips like water clear,
Flowing past, yet always near.
In the stillness, truths unfold,
Within the depths, all stories told.

Emblems of Frost

Morning breaks with icy breath,
Emblems of frost, a spell of death.
Patterns weaving on the glass,
Whispers of the night that pass.

Cold fingers trace a fragile line,
Artistry of nature divine.
Each delicate crystal forms,
Nature's magic, soft and warm.

Trees adorned with jeweled crowns,
Silent witnesses, nature's frowns.
In the chill, a beauty glows,
From the frost, our wonder grows.

Winter's breath, a chilling kiss,
In the stillness, find your bliss.
Emblems of frost, time stands still,
Nature whispers, hearts can fill.

Whispering Snowflakes

Whispers dance upon the breeze,
Softly falling through the trees.
Each flake tells a tale of old,
In silence, secrets yet untold.

They blanket earth in purest white,
Transforming day into the night.
Gentle touch upon the ground,
In their grace, peace can be found.

Crystalline dreams that softly gleam,
In twilight's hush, a fleeting dream.
Laughter echoes, pure and clear,
As winter whispers, drawing near.

In the still, the world inhales,
As time slows down, and magic sails.
Each flake a wish, a tiny spark,
Lighting up the endless dark.

The Stillness Between Storms

A hush drapes o'er the waking morn,
In quietude a day is born.
The air is thick with latent light,
Embracing all, both day and night.

Trees stand tall, a solemn watch,
While whispers fade, the winds will not botch.
Birds rest low, their songs subdued,
In the stillness, time eludes.

Clouds drift lazily overhead,
As peace reigns where chaos tread.
The world prepares for what's to come,
As hearts beat soft, like gentle drums.

In each shadow a promise lays,
Of brighter skies and sunny rays.
Breathe in deep, let worries part,
The stillness mends a weary heart.

Frosted Dreams

Upon the glass, a pattern weaves,
A tapestry of frozen leaves.
Midnight whispers in shimm'ring hues,
Crafting visions that sing the blues.

Gentle touches, sighs so light,
Painted softly, boughs in white.
Every flake a fleeting chance,
To awaken dreams, and set them dance.

Cold embraces, yet warms the heart,
In frosted light, we find our art.
Through winter's breath, we shall ignite,
The flames of hope, burning bright.

Under starlit skies, we roam,
Finding solace, calling it home.
Each dream a star, each wish a flame,
In frosted worlds, we stake our claim.

Where Shadows Lie

In velvet dusk, shadows entwine,
Lost in silence, intricate design.
Echoes dance beneath the trees,
A symphony carried in the breeze.

Forgotten paths beneath the night,
Lead to dreams hidden from sight.
In these corners, secrets dwell,
Where whispered tales of ages tell.

Beneath the moon's soft, silver glow,
The world breathes deep, its pulse slow.
Here in the stillness, hearts align,
In the shaded refuge, pure and fine.

Colors shift in twilight's grace,
Casting shadows on this place.
Listen closely, hear the sighs,
In the dark, where shadows lie.

Muffled Earth

Silence blankets the ground,
Whispers of nature abound.
Footprints vanish with the light,
The world feels cozy and tight.

In the chill of the night air,
Stars twinkle with a rare flair.
Moonlight dances on the snow,
A soft glow where shadows flow.

Branches bow with frozen grace,
Nature wears a tranquil face.
Every sound seems far away,
Time drifts slowly, come what may.

Inside homes, the fires glow,
As winds outside gently blow.
Warmth surrounds every heart,
Together we shall not part.

In this hushed, enchanted space,
Dreams float by in perfect pace.
Muffled earth, we do embrace,
As winter grants its sweet grace.

Snowbound Reverie

Snowflakes waltz through the air,
Nature whispers a cold prayer.
Branches heavy, dressed in white,
The world gleams with pure delight.

Quiet moments drape the land,
Footsteps soft on silken sand.
Children laugh, their breath a mist,
In this winter wonderland twist.

Cocoa warms the weary soul,
In the hearth, the flames roll.
Gentle stories fill the night,
Wrapped in blankets, holding tight.

Dreams cast out on snowy hills,
Sleds and joy bring endless thrills.
Stars above begin to shine,
Each moment feels so divine.

In this snowbound reverie,
Nature holds its symphony.
Time stands still, with love we know,
In this magic, softly glow.

Crystals of Time

Icicles hang like glass shards,
Nature weaves in hushed regards.
Each flake falls with a soft sigh,
A fleeting moment passing by.

Frozen whispers in the trees,
Dance upon the chilly breeze.
Memories held in crystal light,
A timeless beauty in the night.

Time slows down, we breathe it in,
Moments bright, where dreams begin.
Glistening paths lead us away,
To where shadows softly play.

Gathered warmth by flickering flame,
We find joy in winter's game.
Stories shared, some old, some new,
In this magic, hearts are true.

Crystals gleam upon the frost,
Every memory, never lost.
In the silence, peace unfolds,
A treasure trove of memories told.

Beneath a Shroud of Snow

Beneath a shroud, the world lies still,
Silent echoes, time to fill.
Softly wrapped in nature's care,
Winter blankets everywhere.

Every branch adorned in white,
A canvas pure, a soothing sight.
Footsteps muffled, dreams arise,
In the stillness, hearts become wise.

Frosted windows, tales of yore,
Whispers of the life before.
Each breath visible in the cold,
Stories waiting to be told.

As night falls, the stars gleam bright,
A galaxy in winter's light.
Starlit paths guide us along,
In this shroud, we find our song.

Underneath this snow so deep,
Nature guards the dreams we keep.
Embraced by winter's gentle hand,
A serene, enchanted land.

Silenced Symphony

Strings of twilight softly play,
Whispers lost in twilight's sway.
Notes that linger, drift and fade,
In the dark, the dreams are laid.

Echoes dance in muted air,
Faintest sighs filled with despair.
Melodies entwined in night,
Fleeting shadows, hidden light.

In the silence, feelings grow,
Tales of love we used to know.
Hope and longing intertwined,
In this silence, I am blind.

Time stands still, a ghostly bliss,
Moments pass, I feel your kiss.
Yet the music plays no more,
Only silence at the core.

The Canvas of Frost

Morning breaks with glistening light,
Nature's art, a splendid sight.
Each leaf wears a crystal gown,
A frozen tale on golden brown.

With every breath, a cloud appears,
Whispers held within the years.
Painted whispers, soft and rare,
Frosted dreams hang in the air.

Underneath the icy veil,
Life's adventures softly sail.
Footprints mark this wintry trail,
Stories known, yet few unveil.

As the sun begins to rise,
Colors dance in bright disguise.
Frosty hues and shadows merge,
In this moment, hearts emerge.

Emptiness Entwined

A hollow space, a vacant room,
Where echoes linger, thoughts consume.
Silken threads of memory weave,
In the stillness, hearts believe.

Voices fade, like shadows grown,
Where once was laughter, now alone.
Emptiness wraps in soft embrace,
Quietude, a haunting grace.

Stars that flicker in the night,
Whisper tales of lost delight.
Filling voids with silent screams,
In this darkness, dwell my dreams.

Yet amidst the ache, I find,
A fragile hope that sparks the mind.
In the emptiness, I gaze,
Flickers of light through endless haze.

The Sound of Falling Snow

Softly drapes the world in white,
Covering all, both day and night.
Gentle whispers, silent flight,
Snowflakes dance in pure delight.

With each flake, a story falls,
Nature's hush, as evening calls.
Curtains drawn, the stillness glows,
Wrapped in warmth, the beauty grows.

Laughter echoes, children play,
In the snow, we find our way.
Footsteps crunch on winter's floor,
Every sound, a love encore.

As stars twinkle in the cold,
Wonders of the night unfold.
The sound of snow, a pure refrain,
Whispers of joy amidst the rain.

Serenity in the Storm

Winds howl like lost souls,
Amid the raging tempest.
Yet in the heart's quiet,
Calm whispers find their rest.

Lightning paints the night sky,
With flashes fierce and bright.
But beneath the chaos,
Hope flickers in its light.

The world may bend and sway,
In a dance so wild,
Yet peace can be found,
In nature's tempest child.

Raindrops fall like music,
On leaves so green and lush.
In every storm's embrace,
Is the promise of the hush.

When clouds begin to part,
And dawn warms the cold earth,
Serenity blooms bright,
In the storm's silent birth.

Veils of Ice

Underneath the pale moon,
Fields sparkle pure and white.
Veils of ice envelop,
A world wrapped up tight.

Frozen branches glisten,
Hung low with winter's breath.
In silence they are speaking,
Of beauty born from death.

Footsteps crunch on the surface,
Every sound a soft sigh.
Nature's frozen whispers,
Beneath a cobalt sky.

The stars are bright above,
In a shimmer so divine.
Each flake tells a story,
In this grand design.

Though the chill may linger,
And the days feel severe,
Veils of ice remind us,
Spring will soon be here.

The Pause of Nature

In the hush of twilight,
Nature holds her breath.
The world is wrapped in stillness,
A moment's sweet caress.

Birds find their quiet nests,
As the sun dips low.
Shadows stretch and linger,
In the softening glow.

The brook slows its rushing,
To listen to the night.
The trees shake off their worries,
In the fading light.

Every creature settles,
In the sacred pause.
Life takes a deep moment,
To honor nature's laws.

And in this gentle stillness,
Love fills the evening air.
The universe remember,
To always be aware.

Silent Footprints

Footprints in the sand,
A trace of where we've been.
Waves kiss the shoreline,
Whispers soft, serene.

Each step tells a story,
Of laughter, love, and tears.
Carved in grains of wisdom,
Echoes of our years.

With every tide receding,
Memories drift away.
Yet the heart keeps a record,
Of moments by the bay.

The footprints fade to nothing,
But their essence remains.
In the rhythm of the ocean,
Life's dance still sustains.

So walk upon this journey,
With grace and gentle care.
For every silent footprint,
Leaves love upon the air.

The Breath of the Frozen Ground

Beneath a layer, secrets lie,
Whispers of soil, beneath the sky.
A world asleep in icy grace,
Nature holds its wistful face.

Silent tones of muted earth,
Crystals gleam, a tale of birth.
Starlit nights, the shadows play,
Frozen moments, stillness sway.

Roots intertwine in winter's clutch,
Each heartbeat, a gentle touch.
Memories linger, cool and deep,
The frozen ground, a dream to keep.

Time drifts slowly, a sacred pause,
Underneath the frost, a cause.
Life awakens, beneath the cold,
The breath of spring, yet to unfold.

Nature whispers, soft and low,
In frozen silence, life still flows.
A canvas bare, yet full of dreams,
The breath of the ground, a gentle scheme.

Hibernation's Embrace

In the heart of winter's night,
Creatures find their small delight.
Wrapped in warmth, the world outside,
Hibernation, nature's guide.

Softly curled in cozy nooks,
The tale of life in secret books.
Dreams woven with the snows of time,
In stillness safe, their hearts will rhyme.

The earth sleeps with a silent sigh,
Beneath the stars, the moon stands high.
Every heartbeat counts the hours,
As frost blankets hidden flowers.

Awake, the time will come anew,
As spring brings forth the vibrant hue.
For now, in peace, they rest and play,
In hibernation's warm array.

The world outside may chill and freeze,
But in their slumber, all is ease.
Nature whispers softly, sweet,
Hibernation, a slow heartbeat.

Solstice Reverie

Underneath the longest night,
Stars gather in the soft twilight.
A dance of shadows, bright and bold,
Solstice whispers, stories told.

The fire's glow, a warming cheer,
Echoes of laughter draw us near.
In the circle, voices rise,
Dreams take shape beneath the skies.

Nature pauses, breath held tight,
Waiting for the dawn's first light.
In the stillness, hope ignites,
Solstice magic, endless nights.

The wheel of time begins to turn,
In every heart, a flicker burns.
Embrace the dark, let spirits soar,
Within the stillness, find much more.

The lengthening days, a tender gift,
As seasons change and spirits lift.
A reverie, so sweet and free,
Solstice shines with possibility.

Frost's Gentle Caress

Morning dew on blades of grass,
Frost's touch makes the moments pass.
Silken whispers, quiet grace,
Nature dons her crystal lace.

Each breath clouds in crisp, cool air,
A fleeting beauty, rare and fair.
Icicles hang like dreams of night,
In frost's gentle, silver light.

Pine trees wear their snowy hats,
Landscapes dressed in winter's mats.
Beneath the chill, a pulse remains,
A secret dance in frosty veins.

The sun will rise, its warmth will break,
Awakening from winter's ache.
Yet for now, we hold this space,
Embracing frost's gentle caress.

Whispers shared in silent moments,
Wrapped in beauty, nature's components.
A world adorned, both stark and bright,
In frost's embrace, we find the light.

Chilling Emptiness

In the quiet of night, shadows creep,
Lonely whispers of dreams, too deep.
A vacant heart with icy breath,
Yearning for warmth, afraid of death.

Silent echoes of laughter fade,
Memories linger in a dark shade.
Emptiness wrapped in silver light,
A haunting waltz through the still night.

Cold winds carry the weight of despair,
Frosted branches stand stiff and bare.
The world sleeps under a ghostly shroud,
In the chill of void, no voice is loud.

Stars above, distant and bright,
Hidden secrets in the veil of night.
Amidst the silence, a heart once bold,
Sinks deeper into the numbing cold.

Yet in this emptiness, hope may glow,
A flicker of warmth amidst the snow.
In the darkness, a spark may arise,
To melt the frost, and light the skies.

Secrets in the Snow

Underneath the blanket so white,
Whispers of secrets take flight.
Footprints hidden, stories untold,
Nature's parchment, silent, cold.

Each flake that dances through the air,
Carries whispers of those who care.
A world transformed in soft repose,
Wrapped in silence, layered in prose.

The trees are draped in a snowy gown,
Guarding each secret, wearing a crown.
Frozen tales from ages past,
In the cold embrace, memories cast.

Quiet moments held in the freeze,
A breath of magic, a gentle breeze.
In the frost, the heart learns to trust,
To find the warmth hidden in the dust.

As daylight breaks with a golden hue,
The secrets shimmer, soft and new.
In each snowflake, a promise lies,
Waiting for hearts to open their eyes.

Echoes of Hushed Moments

In the stillness, whispers blend,
Time pauses as moments suspend.
Gentle shadows dance and sway,
Echoes linger at close of day.

Fleeting glances, a secret share,
In the silence, a world laid bare.
Soft heartbeats, synchronized sighs,
In laughter's echo, love never dies.

Captured smiles in fading light,
Dreams entwined through the endless night.
Cherished echoes, soft and sweet,
Moments stilled, life finds its beat.

In the twilight, a tender glance,
Time unfolds in a silent dance.
Hushed moments weave a sacred thread,
Binding souls, where hearts are led.

As stars emerge, the echoes play,
Filling the night, chasing fears away.
In the quiet, dreams come alive,
In the hush, love learns to thrive.

The Veil of Frost

Morning dew in a silver lace,
Cloaks the world in a gentle embrace.
A veil of frost on every seed,
Whispers of winter, a timeless creed.

Windows glisten, a magical frame,
Capturing nature's quiet game.
Branches adorned with icy jewels,
Nature's artistry, beauty fuels.

Beneath the frost, life holds its breath,
Waiting patiently for spring's caress.
Hidden warmth, a promise awakes,
In silence, the spirit gently shakes.

Rays of sun break the morning chill,
Melting whispers, the heartbeats still.
Each droplet dances, a fleeting song,
Reminding us where we all belong.

In the twilight, as shadows creep,
The frost draws close, holding secrets deep.
In every corner, a story told,
In the veil of frost, life unfolds.

The Dance of Winter Stars

In the velvet sky they gleam,
Stars twirl in a silent dream,
Whispers of a frosty night,
Wrapped in shimmering light.

Snowflakes fall like gentle sighs,
Kissing earth beneath dark skies,
Each one unique, pure, and clear,
Nature's lace so soft, sincere.

The moon casts shadows long and wide,
While winter's chill becomes our guide,
Step carefully on the frozen ground,
In this peaceful realm, solace found.

A dance of lights in the inky sea,
Invite the heart to wander free,
As constellations tell their tales,
Of ancient journeys, love prevails.

Breathe in the magic, the crisp, fresh air,
Feel the wonder, warmth, and care,
With every step, let joy ignite,
In the dance of stars, pure delight.

Peaceful Isolation of Snow

Snow blankets the world in white,
Hushes sounds, brings quiet night,
Each flake settles, soft and slow,
In this tranquil, wondrous glow.

Trees adorned in crystal coats,
Whispers float on chilly moats,
Branches bow, a graceful bend,
Nature's art, no need to tend.

Footprints fade, a fleeting trace,
In solitude, I find my place,
With every breath, silence deep,
In this peace, my spirit leaps.

Icicles hang like silver tears,
Stories etched of winter years,
In isolation, I find grace,
Embracing the cold's warm embrace.

As twilight falls, the stars appear,
A lullaby of night draws near,
In the peaceful isolation, I know,
That beauty blooms in falling snow.

The Art of Stillness

In quiet corners shadows play,
A whisper lingers, soft and gray.
The world outside begins to fade,
In silent peace, the heart is made.

Time gently slows, the breath is light,
In stillness found, we find our sight.
Thoughts like leaves in autumn sway,
In moments hushed, we lose our way.

The hum of life, a distant tune,
Within this space, we learn to bloom.
Each heartbeat echoes with the trees,
In sacred calm, the soul finds ease.

Glimmers of hope through quiet streams,
In solitude, we chase our dreams.
The art of stillness, a tender grace,
In silence, we embrace our place.

Moonlit Solitude

Beneath the stars, a world so bright,
The moon casts shadows in soft light.
Each moment draped in silver hue,
In whispered night, the heart feels true.

Gentle breezes touch the skin,
A dance of dreams where thoughts begin.
Alone yet whole, in peace we tread,
The night unfolds, our fears are shed.

Reflections glow on waters wide,
In solitude, the soul's a guide.
The silver beams, a tender glow,
In moonlit paths, we learn to grow.

Wandering thoughts like clouds on high,
In quiet moments, we can fly.
With every breath, the heart expands,
In moonlit solitude, love stands.

Waking the Sleeping Earth

With dawn's embrace, the world awakes,
From slumber deep, the silence breaks.
A gentle stir, the flowers rise,
Beneath the sun, the heart complies.

The trees stand tall, their limbs outspread,
In vibrant hues, the colors thread.
The songs of birds fill morning air,
In waking life, we shed despair.

Fresh dew glistens on emerald blades,
Through fragrant blooms, the light cascades.
Each breath a gift, the day unfolds,
With every moment, beauty molds.

Nature's pulse begins to hum,
A rhythmic beat, the day will come.
In waking earth, our spirits lift,
In every pause, we find our gift.

Echoes in the Cold

Through icy winds, a whisper flows,
In frozen depths, the soft heart knows.
The world in white, a canvas bare,
In echoes lost, we hear the air.

Each footprint left in powdery snow,
Tells tales of time, of ebb and flow.
In chilling breath, the silence speaks,
In stillness found, the spirit seeks.

Winter's grasp, both harsh and sweet,
In every glance, the cold's heartbeat.
With frosty nights, the stars are bold,
In echoes deep, our dreams unfold.

Beneath the moon, the shadows blend,
In quiet night, we find a friend.
Through echoing breezes, hearts grow warm,
In winter's hold, we find our form.

The Quiet of Falling Snowflakes

In the stillness, whispers glide,
Snowflakes dance, they gently hide.
Silence wraps the world around,
In this hush, peace is found.

Each flake unique, a wondrous art,
Softly drifting, they play their part.
Blankets of white, a tranquil sheet,
The earth sleeps under the icy beat.

Footsteps muffled, paths unclear,
A world transformed, so pure, so near.
Nature's hush, a soft embrace,
In falling snow, we find our grace.

Frosty breath, the air's delight,
Twinkling stars in the velvet night.
Moments linger, hearts so free,
In winter's hold, we just can be.

Holding secrets, the snowfall weaves,
A tapestry of dreams it leaves.
Quiet magic, beneath the sky,
In falling snow, our spirits fly.

Glistening Breath of the Earth

Morning dew like diamonds shines,
Nature wakes and softly aligns.
Every leaf, a sparkling gem,
Life anew, a sacred hymn.

Sunlight kisses the vibrant green,
A glistening realm, pure and serene.
Colors burst, a vivid show,
In this breath, the earth will glow.

Gentle winds caress the trees,
A symphony in the soft breeze.
Whispers dance, secrets shared,
Soul of nature, tenderly cared.

In every petal, life's essence found,
Rhythms of earth, a sacred sound.
Together with the sky so bright,
A world alive in morning light.

Moments captured, fleeting yet clear,
Glistening breath, so pure, so near.
Embrace the day, let the heart sway,
In nature's arms, we long to stay.

Shadows in the Frost

Beneath the moon, shadows creep,
In the frost, secrets keep.
Figures linger, silent, bold,
Stories wrapped in the night's cold hold.

Whispers echo through the trees,
Chill of winter in the breeze.
Shadows dance with every breath,
A ballet of life, together with death.

Footprints lost in the shimmering sheen,
Paths forgotten, yet to be seen.
Silent watch of the stars above,
Guarding the mysteries we dare to love.

Twilight cloaks the world in white,
A canvas painted in soft moonlight.
From the shadows, dreams arise,
Glowing softly like distant skies.

In the frost, we weave our fate,
In silence, hearts contemplate.
Amidst the chill, our hopes ignite,
Shadows linger, yet spirits take flight.

The Softness of Frozen Air

A breath of winter, crisp and clear,
Fills the heart, drawing near.
Each inhale, a moment slowed,
In frozen air, our stories glow.

Silken whispers, the world confined,
Gentle stillness, peace entwined.
Frosted branches, a delicate lace,
Nature's wonder, a sacred space.

Clouds drift softly in the sky,
Silent echoes, a gentle sigh.
Every chill, a tender kiss,
In frozen air, we find our bliss.

With every exhale, we release,
Layers peel, finding peace.
In the silence, hearts align,
Bound together, yours and mine.

The softness wraps, a warm embrace,
In winter's breath, we find our place.
Connected to earth, we float and sway,
In the frozen air, we choose to stay.

Calm before the Thaw

The winter's breath holds tight,
Quiet whispers fill the night.
Buds are dreaming beneath the snow,
Awaiting warmth, the sun's soft glow.

A stillness drapes the frozen land,
Nature waits, a patient hand.
In this silence, hope will grow,
A promise seen in melting flow.

Icicles hang like crystal spears,
Time stands still, it calms our fears.
Yet, soon the warmth will break the cold,
Revealing secrets yet untold.

As days grow longer, shadows fade,
The landscape shifts, the game is played.
A tapestry of life will weave,
In every heart, the joy to believe.

So let us breathe this peaceful air,
Embrace the stillness, show we care.
For in this calm, the world will thaw,
Prepare to bloom, the spring's sweet awe.

Shadows on a Snowy Path

Shadows dance in twilight's glow,
Footprints mark where we shall go.
Whispers soft of winter's breath,
A haunting touch of life and death.

The trees stand tall, their branches bare,
Cloaked in white, a winter's flair.
Beneath the snow, life still resides,
Hidden dreams where magic hides.

Each crunch below, a tale unfolds,
Stories woven, time retold.
The moonlight casts a silver sheen,
On paths where hearts have always been.

A flicker here, a shadow there,
Moments linger in the air.
Through snowy fields, we walk in peace,
As winter's grip begins to cease.

And when we reach the forest's end,
New journeys wait, our hearts will mend.
With every step, we shed the past,
Embracing warmth that comes at last.

Where Quiet Dreams Whisper

In the hush of silent nights,
Where dreams take flight, and lanterns bright.
The stars above, a guide so clear,
Whispering secrets, soft and near.

Gentle breezes brush my face,
In this tranquil, sacred space.
Thoughts drift like clouds, so far away,
In quiet dreams, we long to stay.

A world unfolds beyond our eyes,
Mysteries tucked in velvet skies.
With every breath, enchantments flow,
Embracing all we come to know.

Where shadows play and fires glow,
Echoes linger from long ago.
The heart finds solace, peace, and flame,
In whispered dreams, there lies no shame.

So close your eyes and drift with me,
To places where the wild things be.
In every heartbeat, let it gleam,
For life is but a fleeting dream.

The Whispering Drift

Winds are calling through the trees,
Carrying tales upon the breeze.
A soft embrace, a gentle sigh,
The whispering drift is passing by.

Snowflakes swirl in a graceful dance,
Nature's art, a fleeting chance.
Each flake unique, a tale of its own,
A drop of beauty, the seeds have sown.

Footsteps muffled on the ground,
In this stillness, peace is found.
Moments linger, time stands still,
A breath of magic, a heart to fill.

The sky above begins to fade,
Golden hues in twilight laid.
As shadows stretch, and stars ignite,
We find our way back to the light.

Together here, beneath the sky,
In the drift where secrets lie.
With every whisper, we transcend,
To the edge of night, where dreams ascend.

In the Grip of a Blue Hour

The sky drapes soft in deeper hues,
Whispers of twilight, cool and muse.
Shadows dance under fading light,
The world holds its breath, cloaked in night.

Night blooms with stars, a distant glow,
Moon serenades the earth below.
In silence, secrets softly breathe,
As time melts away, heartstrings weave.

A moment caught, the dusk unfurls,
Painting dreams with muted swirls.
Each sigh lingers, a fleeting trace,
In the blue hour, we find our space.

Reflections ripple on the lake,
As if the world begins to wake.
Soft hues cradle the weary heart,
In stillness, we find our art.

The sky will blush, the night will wane,
Yet in this hour, joy remains.
Captured softly, like a prayer,
In the grip of blue, we lose our care.

Traces in the Snow

A blanket white on fields so bare,
Whispers quiet through the air.
Each footprint tells a tale of old,
Imprints gentle, stories unfold.

The trees stand tall, wrapped in frost,
Remembering moments that were lost.
Bare branches reach for heaven's grace,
In winter's hush, we find our place.

Snowflakes dance on a winter's breeze,
Each one unique, they swirl with ease.
Nature's canvas, pure and bright,
Where echoes linger, lost in flight.

As silence falls, the world at rest,
Every flake, a lover's jest.
In this stillness, the heart will know,
The warmth hidden beneath the snow.

With every storm that sweeps the ground,
Life's fragile beauty can be found.
In traces left, a sacred vow,
A promise whispered in the now.

A Pause in the Breath of Earth

The mountains sigh, a tranquil scene,
In stillness held, where time is keen.
Rivers pause in the gentle light,
As nature cradles day and night.

Whispers brush through the leafy trees,
Carried softly on the breeze.
In the hush, the heart can mend,
With every sound, a sweet descend.

Clouds drift lazily across the sky,
A dance of shadows, low and high.
In the silence, dreams take flight,
Painting hope with strokes of light.

Each breath we take, a shared delight,
In harmony, holding tight.
Pause a moment, let it be,
In earth's embrace, we're wild and free.

A sacred space where time slows down,
In every heartbeat, wear no crown.
With nature's grace, find what it's worth,
In that pause, the breath of earth.

Where Time Stands Still

Amidst the trees, in shadows deep,
Secrets linger, dreams we keep.
A golden hour, the sun's last kiss,
In stillness found, we find our bliss.

The river flows in timeless grace,
Reflecting worlds, a soft embrace.
Leaves rustle tales of ages past,
In every moment, forever cast.

Clouds hang low, heavy with dreams,
Time unwinds, or so it seems.
In whispers soft, the earth reveals,
The quiet truth that gently heals.

With every breath, the world does sway,
In this stillness, night meets day.
Here in the quiet, hearts may thrill,
In the magic where time stands still.

So linger long, let worries fade,
In the silence, a serenade.
For in that space, we lose the chase,
In stillness found, we find our place.

Beneath the Snowy Canopy

Whispers dance through branches high,
Blanketed in white, they sigh.
Stars peer from their velvet night,
Nature sleeps, bathed in light.

Footprints trace the quiet ground,
Secrets in the silence found.
A world wrapped in crystal grace,
Time slows down in this embrace.

Frozen breaths in frosty air,
Echoes linger everywhere.
Beneath the boughs, dreams take flight,
Guided by the silver light.

Crisp and clear, the echoes wane,
Promises like gentle rain.
In this hush, all fears dissolve,
Within the snow, our hearts evolve.

The night deepens, shadows blend,
Whispers tell of journeys' end.
Beneath the snowy canopy,
A world awaits, wild and free.

The Sigh of Slumbering Nature

In the hush of twilight's glow,
Nature breathes in softest flow.
Mountains draped in gentle mist,
In this realm, no dreams are missed.

A river flows with tranquil grace,
Reflecting all, a perfect space.
Stars emerge, the sky alight,
The sigh of night, embracing tight.

Crickets hum a lullaby,
As the wind begins to sigh.
Wrapped in layers, warm and deep,
Nature falls into her sleep.

The moonlight spills on fields of green,
Golden hues in silver sheen.
Every creature finds its rest,
In this moment, truly blessed.

Time stands still, a fleeting art,
In the quiet, feel the heart.
The sigh of slumbering nature,
Whispers softly, pure and sure.

Calm After the Flurry

Snowflakes twirl, a wild dance,
Whirling fast, they take their chance.
With a hush, the storm will fade,
Leaving whispers, soft cascade.

In the stillness, peace is found,
Gentle silence wraps around.
Footprints mark the world anew,
In the calm, the hope breaks through.

Branches bow with heavy coat,
Shimmering like dreams afloat.
Every flake a tale to tell,
Of the storm where chaos dwelled.

Rays of sun begin to shine,
Melting shadows, drawing line.
Colors burst, a vibrant show,
In this calm, the world will glow.

Nature breathes, a gentle sigh,
Painting beauty in the sky.
Calm after the flurry's flight,
Brings a world of pure delight.

Frosty Reverie

Morning light breaks, crisp and clear,
Frosty breath, a chill draws near.
Windows frost, like dreams in hue,
Whispers of the ice-kissed blue.

Every blade adorned with lace,
Nature dons a frozen grace.
Beneath the sky, a dance unfolds,
Frosty tales in silence told.

Pines stand tall in coats of white,
Guardians of the winter night.
In their shadow, secrets hide,
Frosty whispers, dreams abide.

Rivers sleep beneath the ice,
Holding time in stillness, nice.
Every echo, soft and sweet,
In the frosty reverie, we meet.

As the sun begins to rise,
Glistening beneath open skies.
Frosty moments, pure and rare,
In this magic, we are there.

The Quiet of the Hearth

By flickering fire, shadows dance,
Whispers float in soft romance,
Warmth embraces every breath,
In this corner, fear meets death.

The logs crackle, stories take flight,
Radiating warmth against the night,
Glimmers of a golden glow,
Crafting peace in the hearth's flow.

Cups clink gently, laughter shared,
In this moment, souls prepared,
To treasure time, to simply be,
In the quiet, hearts roam free.

Togetherness ignites the space,
Comfort found in each embrace,
Here, with love, the world takes pause,
In the hearth's soft, loving cause.

As embers fade, dusk will call,
Still, our spirits shall not fall,
For in this warmth, we'll ever stay,
In the quiet, come what may.

Embrace of the Frost

Branches glisten, silver threads,
Nature dons her jeweled spreads.
Whispers echo through the trees,
Embrace the chill upon the breeze.

Footprints crunch on winter's ground,
In this frozen silence found,
Every breath forms clouds of white,
Underneath the pale moonlight.

Stars peek through the crystal veil,
In this stillness, all hearts sail,
Warmed by dreams of spring's return,
Yet in frost, our spirits burn.

A quiet moment, nature's prayer,
Beauty rests, suspended air,
Each flake falls, a dance of grace,
In the frost, we find our place.

With every dawn, the frost will fade,
But in our hearts, the chill will wade,
Embrace the frost, let silence reign,
In winter's grasp, there's joy and pain.

Crystal-Crowned Stillness

Morning breaks with whispered light,
Crystals crown the world in white.
Every branch a gleaming jewel,
In this calm, the heart's a fool.

Watching closely, breath held tight,
Nature's beauty, pure delight.
Sunlight dances on frosted leaves,
As the world outside believes.

A moment's pause, serene and sweet,
In this stillness, hearts entreat,
To grasp the magic of the day,
With crystal crowns, we gently play.

Winter's kiss upon our sight,
In this peace, the world feels right.
Every glimmer, a fleeting chance,
In nature's crystal, we find romance.

As daylight wanes, shadows crew,
Fading whispers bid adieu,
But in our hearts, the stillness stays,
Crystal-crowned, in endless ways.

The Beauty of Absence

In empty spaces, silence reigns,
Echoes linger, pierce like chains.
Memories twirl, a distant song,
In absence, we find where we belong.

Each moment missed, like fleeting dusk,
In shadows, whispers form a husk,
Yet beauty blooms in vacant air,
In every ache, there lies a care.

Fragmented dreams, a tender trace,
In absence, we unearth the grace.
Fading laughter, softly spoken,
In the silence, hearts unbroken.

With every breath, the void expands,
Still, we hold what love commands.
For in the stillness, truth is born,
The beauty of absence, never worn.

And when the heart begins to heal,
We find the strength in what is real.
For absence teaches, gently flows,
In every path, a flower grows.

Crystal Gardens of Quietude

In the still of night, they gleam,
Crystal petals in a dream.
Silent whispers, soft and clear,
Nature's magic lingers near.

Moonlight dances on the dew,
Sparkling gems in shades of blue.
Every shadow breathes a sigh,
In this garden, time slips by.

The air is filled with gentle peace,
Each moment feels like a release.
Crystals glow with tranquil light,
Guiding hearts through endless night.

Wander softly, take your time,
Feel the rhythm, sense the rhyme.
In this haven, lose your cares,
Wrapped in beauty, no one's there.

As the dawn begins to creep,
Stars fade gently, fall asleep.
Yet the memory lingers still,
In crystal gardens, hearts can heal.

The Breath of the Deep Freeze

In the depth of winter's breath,
Silence reigns where life meets death.
Frosted pines stand tall and proud,
Shrouded in their icy shroud.

Fields lie blanketed in white,
Moonlit whispers, cold and bright.
Every step is soft and slow,
Time is caught in winter's flow.

Brittle air sings crisp and clear,
Echoing the chill we fear.
Yet beneath the frozen skin,
Life awaits to breathe again.

When the thaw begins to start,
Trembles gently in the heart.
Springtime's song shall soon appear,
Bringing warmth, dispelling fear.

So let winter take its hold,
In its grasp, the world turns gold.
For in cold's embrace, we find,
A secret strength in frost entwined.

Sighs of Ancient Trees

Whispers ride the gentle breeze,
Rustling through the ancient trees.
Every trunk holds tales of old,
Secrets in their bark unfold.

Roots that reach into the past,
Witness to the shadows cast.
Branches stretch with grace and might,
Cradling dreams in soft twilight.

Leaves that shimmer, tales to tell,
Echoes of a time they dwell.
In their sighs, the stories weave,
Nature's breath that won't deceive.

Underneath the leafy shade,
Resting souls in peace are laid.
Tiny creatures find their home,
Among the boughs where wild things roam.

Listen closely, hear the sound,
Of nature's wisdom all around.
In the sighs of ancient trees,
Lie the whispers of the breeze.

Sleep of the Earth

Underneath a velvet night,
Earth is wrapped in slumber tight.
Mountains cradle, valleys sigh,
Stars above like watchful eyes.

Rivers whisper calm and low,
Carrying secrets down below.
Quiet hills and fields are still,
Wrapped in nature's gentle will.

Every creature seeks its rest,
Nestled safe, in cozy nest.
Life takes pause, a moment sweet,
In the arms of night's heartbeat.

Dreams are spun in softest light,
Painting shadows with delight.
In this stillness, tales unfold,
A lullaby for hearts so bold.

Come the dawn, the world will wake,
A fresh beginning, for us to take.
But for now, let silence reign,
In the Earth's embrace, true peace we gain.

Cold Moonlight's Embrace

In the stillness of night,
Moonlight casts its gentle glow.
Whispers dance on the cool air,
Wrap me in silver shadows.

A world bathed in soft light,
Where the heart learns to listen.
Every breath a sweet promise,
In the night's tender embrace.

Trees sway in quiet harmony,
Rustling leaves tell ancient tales.
The sky, a vast canvas bright,
Painted with dreams and secrets.

Beneath this celestial dome,
I find solace in the dark.
Each star a distant beacon,
Guiding my wandering thoughts.

Cold moonlight, forever near,
Cradles the world in its arms.
In this tranquil serenity,
I am at peace, I am whole.

Crystals of Quiet Reflection

Morning dew on blades of grass,
Glimmers like diamonds in the sun.
Each drop a moment frozen,
A world in perfect stillness.

The air is crisp and unbroken,
Nature sings a silent hymn.
In this quietude I wander,
Finding joy in the small things.

Time slows down to pulse softly,
As shadows stretch and yawn wide.
In the depths of calm I see,
The beauty of life's simple gifts.

Every breath invites wonder,
Every glance shares a story.
The heart beats in calm rhythm,
Echoing the world around.

Crystals form in thoughts lingering,
Reflections of moments cherished.
In this peace I embrace all,
Finding grace in still waters.

When the World Turns White

Snowflakes fall in silent grace,
Blanketing the earth below.
A soft hush envelops all,
As nature holds its breath tight.

Footsteps crunch on frosty ground,
Whispers carried by the chill.
Each breath steams in the air,
A reminder of warmth within.

Trees stand tall in winter's hold,
Draped in white, like brides at rest.
The landscape painted anew,
Underneath a thickened quilt.

Children laugh and play in snow,
Building dreams from frosted flakes.
Joy spills forth in the cold air,
Warming hearts like fire's glow.

When the world turns white and pure,
It teaches us to pause, reflect.
In this beauty, life is still,
Moments cherished, peace embraced.

The Silence of Stars in Cold

In the depth of starry night,
A blanket of frozen stillness.
Stars twinkle like distant thoughts,
Flickering, yet always near.

The universe whispers softly,
Secrets hidden in its vastness.
Each pinprick of light a wish,
Floating through the darkened sky.

Coldness wraps the world in peace,
A moment to breathe and dream.
The silence is a warm embrace,
Cradling hopes in gentle ways.

Underneath this cosmic dome,
I find solace in the quiet.
In the heart of frozen darkness,
The stars sing songs of comfort.

Though the chill may bite the skin,
Inside glows a flickering fire.
I stand beneath the silent stars,
Filled with wonder, drifting far.

The Stillness That Follows

In the hush of twilight's breath,
Winter cloaks the earth in peace.
Footprints vanish, lost in depth,
Quiet moments never cease.

Branches bend with silver light,
Shadows dance on frozen ground.
Stars emerge to touch the night,
Secrets held, with silence crowned.

Crimson leaves now softly fade,
Whispers fade into the dark.
Nature's beauty, still displayed,
In the night, a gentle spark.

Time stands still, a fleeting breath,
Love is woven through the air.
Life and dreams, not bound by death,
In this stillness, hearts lay bare.

Echoes linger, soft and small,
Memories drift like the snow.
In this moment, we feel all,
In stillness, spirits glow.

Beneath the Starry Frost

A quilt of stars hangs from above,
Twinkling in the chilly night.
Wrapped in peace, as dreams take flight,
The world sleeps, embraced by love.

Frosted breath in moonlit air,
Whispers echo through the trees.
Nature's secrets, calm and rare,
Dance upon the frozen breeze.

Gentle winds caress the ground,
Softly sing their winter song.
In their melody, we're found,
In their harmony, we belong.

Underneath the frosty weave,
Glances exchanged, hearts entwined.
In this dream, we dare believe,
A tranquil world, so undefined.

Peace descends like winter's grace,
In the stillness, shadows play.
Beneath the sky's vast, velvet space,
The heart finds warmth, come what may.

Echoes of the Gentle Cold

Winter whispers to the trees,
Echoing through still and bright.
In the calm, we find the ease,
Of the soft and frosty light.

Crystal flakes begin to fall,
Each a story, pure and old.
Nature heeds the winter call,
Chilling hearts with gentle cold.

Branches glisten, covered white,
In the hush of evening's hush.
Every star a tiny light,
In the cosmos, soft and lush.

Timeless moments flicker past,
Touched by dreams that drift away.
Yet in silence, love will last,
In our hearts, it lights the way.

Echoes fade, but we remain,
Chasing shadows through the night.
In the cold, we feel no pain,
Only warmth in starlit sight.

Subdued Whispers of the Season

A quiet hush fills all the air,
As snowflakes dance in muted light.
Every moment, soft and rare,
Bids farewell to day, goodnight.

Time weaves stories in the frost,
Wrapped in silence, dreams take flight.
In this moment, nothing lost,
Only whispers of delight.

Gentle sighs of winter's breath,
Call to us with soothing grace.
In the chill, we find no death,
But a warm, embracing place.

Footsteps linger in the night,
Each a echo of love's call.
Underneath the starlit sight,
We are held, not lost at all.

Season's shift, like tides of time,
In this stillness, we will stay.
Hand in hand, our hearts will rhyme,
In subdued whispers, come what may.

Murmurs in the Chill Air

Whispers float through winter's night,
A soft caress, pure and light.
Cold breath dances on the pine,
Nature weaves its tale divine.

Silvery stars like scattered dreams,
Glimmer gently, or so it seems.
Winter's chill, an ancient song,
In this quiet, we belong.

Frosted leaves underfoot crackle,
As we share secrets, hearts tackle.
Echoes seized in ghostly air,
Murmurs linger everywhere.

Midnight cloaked in softest shade,
Where shadows play and fears cascade.
Through every chill, warmth can grow,
In this dance, our spirits flow.

So let the night wrap us tight,
In murmurs shared, our souls ignite.
A tapestry of frost and cheer,
In the hush, the world is clear.

In the Embrace of Midnight Blue

Starlit canvas stretched above,
A silent plea, a gentle love.
Midnight whispers secrets true,
Wrapped in shades of deepest blue.

Silver beams on water's face,
Time slows down in this still place.
Crickets sing a soft refrain,
In the night, we feel no pain.

Thoughts drift like clouds at dusk,
In the air, a fading musk.
Each heartbeat echoes in the vast,
The present's glow, the future's cast.

Within this realm of night's embrace,
Fear and doubt find no trace.
Close your eyes and feel the hue,
Life awakens, fresh and new.

Beneath the sky's eternal dome,
In shadows deep, we find our home.
Together in the midnight glow,
With every breath, our spirits flow.

The Stillness that Breathes

Silent echoes fill the air,
Whispers of a world laid bare.
Beneath the hush, a heartbeat thrums,
In stillness, the heartache succumbs.

Gentle breeze through trees does weave,
Nature breathes, oh how we cleave.
Time pauses in the soft embrace,
Fleeting moments we can't replace.

Light dapples the ground below,
In shadows where soft secrets flow.
With every pause, the world stands still,
A space to breathe, a quiet thrill.

In gentle sighs, the dawn will break,
As day awakens without mistake.
Hold the stillness, let it seep,
In sacred silence, dreams we keep.

Find peace within the muted sound,
In stillness, our true selves are found.
The breath of life, a soft caress,
In quietude, we feel blessed.

Unspoken Beauty of the Chill

Frosted mornings offer grace,
A whisper in a sacred space.
Beauty lies in icy glints,
Nature's charm and silent hints.

As twilight settles, shadows play,
In chilling winds, their dance conveys.
Every branch draped in white lace,
Holds stories time can't erase.

Beneath the frost, life pulses strong,
In stillness, we find where we belong.
Winter's breath, a fragile thrill,
In every moment, hearts we fill.

Hold this beauty, sweet and rare,
In soft gazes, we learn to share.
Unspoken bonds, a gentle way,
Through frosty nights and dawns of gray.

In the chill, we find delight,
A world reborn in silver light.
Unveiling truths too long concealed,
In winter's clutch, our hearts are healed.

Frosted Whisper

The morning glows in silver hue,
Soft whispers dance on frosty air.
Each breath a cloud, a gentle cue,
　Nature's hush, a tranquil stare.

Trees adorned with glistening lace,
A frozen world, serene and bright.
Footprints left in quiet grace,
　As day melts softly into night.

The sun ascends, a golden beam,
　Awakening the chill to warm.
In winter's grasp, we dare to dream,
　Finding peace within the storm.

Birds take flight, a fleeting sight,
Their songs echo through stillness wide.
A world transformed in pure delight,
　Where whispers of the frost abide.

As shadows stretch and daylight fades,
　A serene calm begins to grow.
In nature's arms, our worries wade,
　Embraced by whispers of the snow.

Echoes of Stillness

In the hush, the world stands still,
Time drips slowly, like melting ice.
Every heartbeat, a gentle thrill,
Whispers echo in silent spice.

Stars blink softly in velvet skies,
Silhouettes of trees reach high.
The moon reflects in your wise eyes,
While dreams flutter like a sigh.

Clouds drift lazily, floating free,
Embracing night's gentle call.
In the quiet, you and me,
Finding beauty in it all.

The river murmurs, secrets spun,
As shadows dance upon the shore.
In echoes, we become as one,
Capturing stillness evermore.

Each heartbeat forms a tender bond,
In this silence, we reside.
With echoes of moments that respond,
To whispers where our dreams collide.

Hushed Elegy of Snow

Softly falls the silent snow,
A blanket wrapped in whispered grace.
The world beneath begins to glow,
As winter's touch leaves a tender trace.

Each flake unique, a fleeting art,
A dance of white in chilly air.
Within the cold, it warms the heart,
Creating beauty everywhere.

Trees wear coats of frosted white,
Guardians of a world so pure.
In their shadows, dreams take flight,
As stillness reigns, we feel secure.

Beneath the stars, we ponder deep,
The hush enveloping our souls.
In this elegy, we softly creep,
Towards the warmth that winter stole.

As dawn awakens, snowflakes gleam,
Life resumes in shimmering glow.
In hushed reflections, softly dream,
In echoes of the fallen snow.

Veil of Crystal Dreams

Through the mist, a veil appears,
Crafted by the breath of night.
Crystal dreams and hidden fears,
Whisper softly, taking flight.

Nighttime weaves its silver thread,
Stars adorn the canvas high.
In this dance, the heart can tread,
Through dreams that sparkle in the sky.

Moonlight bathes the slumbering earth,
Kissing shadows, soft and pale.
In the stillness, comes rebirth,
As we sail on dreams, set sail.

With each heartbeat, magic glows,
An unseen force both kind and bold.
In the night, our spirit flows,
With dreams as treasures to behold.

As dawn arrives, the veil will part,
Revealing tales of joys and schemes.
In these moments, know my heart,
Forever bound in crystal dreams.

Tranquil Twilight

The sun dips low, a gentle sigh,
Colors blend as day waves goodbye.
Whispers linger in the fading light,
Embracing peace within the night.

Stars begin to twinkle, slow and bright,
Moon casts silver, igniting the night.
Crickets sing their soft serenade,
In twilight's embrace, worries fade.

The shadows stretch, the world feels still,
A tranquil heart, untouched by ill.
The breeze hums low, a soft refrain,
In this quiet, calm remains.

Nature breathes, a gentle pause,
In this moment, we find cause.
To cherish life, to note the beauty,
In twilight's grace, we find our duty.

So let us linger, where silence reigns,
In the twilight glow, where peace remains.
With every heartbeat, feel the flow,
In the tranquil night, let worry go.

Glistening Respite

Beneath the trees, where shadows play,
A shimmering brook brightens the day.
Morning dew on leaves, a silver kiss,
In nature's arms, we find our bliss.

Sunlight dances on the water's face,
A moment stolen in this serene place.
Birds call softly, echoing cheer,
In the glistening light, troubles disappear.

Wildflowers bloom, a vibrant hue,
Whispers of color, nature's view.
Inhaling deeply, the fresh, sweet air,
Finding solace, free from care.

As time unfolds, the world feels new,
In this respite, life's joy breaks through.
With every breath, we stitch our fate,
In this glistening realm, we celebrate.

So let us wander through this bright scene,
Finding peace where nature's been.
In every glimmer, a tale awaits,
In life's gentle flow, love cultivates.

The Quietude of Nature

In the forest deep, where silence reigns,
A tranquil world breaks the chains.
Gentle rustle of leaves in the breeze,
Nature whispers, the heart finds ease.

Mountains stand tall, a sentinel's guard,
Quietude wraps like a soft, warm shard.
The softest murmur of the flowing stream,
In this haven, life feels like a dream.

Mornings unfold in a golden light,
Creatures awaken, taking flight.
The sun spills warmth on the cool, damp earth,
In nature's quiet, we find rebirth.

As shadows lengthen in the fading day,
The dusk brings calm, gently at play.
Every heartbeat sings a sweet tune,
In the stillness, we are attuned.

So let's embrace this sacred peace,
Where nature's wonders never cease.
In the quietude, we find our grace,
In harmony's breath, we trace our place.

Eerie Serenity

Fog creeps in as shadows play,
An eerie whisper marks the day.
Moonlight glints on twisted trees,
A shiver dances with the breeze.

Crickets chirp in a haunting tune,
Beneath a watchful, silver moon.
The night unfolds its silken veil,
In eerie realms, the heart sets sail.

Winds carry tales of ages lost,
In the stillness, we count the cost.
Echoes linger, dreams long gone,
In this twilight, we press on.

Stars blink low, their secrets kept,
In the silence, many have wept.
Yet here we stand, both bold and meek,
In eerie serenity, we seek.

So let the night wrap us like a shroud,
In shadows deep, we'll sing aloud.
Finding beauty in what incites fear,
In the eerie calm, we persevere.

Luminescent Tranquility of Snow

Softly it falls, a blanket of white,
Whispering peace in the still of the night.
Each flake a dream, pure as can be,
Dancing in silence, wild and free.

Moonlight glistens on the frozen ground,
Soft echoes linger, a gentle sound.
Nature's deep breath, a moment to pause,
Wrapped in the magic of winter's cause.

Trees wear coats of crystalline grace,
Time slows down, in this tranquil space.
The world is hushed, as if to reflect,
On beauty that nature does quietly project.

Footprints remain, a fleeting trace,
Of journeys made in this wondrous place.
Under the stars, where dreams are sewn,
In luminescence, we feel not alone.

A World Wrapped in Hush

A soft gray shroud blankets the earth,
Waking the whispers of winter's worth.
Gentle winds murmur, secrets untold,
As silence weaves patterns, tenderly bold.

Frost-kissed branches outline the sky,
While stars wink softly, as night drifts by.
Each breath of cold, a promise to keep,
As the world around slowly falls deep.

Snowflakes drift slowly, in delicate flow,
Embracing the quiet, like time moving slow.
In this soft cocoon, where echoes do fade,
A tranquil heart finds its serenade.

The moon hangs low, a guardian bright,
Guiding the lost through the onset of night.
In the hush of the moment, together we dwell,
In the charm of the silence, we find peace so well.

Refinement of the Frigid

Every corner shimmers in diamond light,
The world adorned in frosty delight.
With each icy breath, nature exhales,
An elegance wrapped in crystalline tales.

Glacial streams murmur beneath the ice,
Winter's embrace feels cool, yet so nice.
Each crystal formed, a story untold,
In the sharpness of air, our senses unfold.

The stars hang low in a velvet sea,
Whispers of warmth, a promise to be.
In this refined moment, hearts intertwine,
Finding solace within the design.

With bated breath, we witness the dawn,
Glistening hills where shadows are drawn.
In the elegance found in dreams and fears,
The frigid air whispers sweetly in our ears.

When Nature Takes a Breath

Stillness descends as the world holds its breath,
An interlude sweet, the calm after death.
In the hush, we sense the pulse of the earth,
Like a lullaby sung, a moment of worth.

Snowflakes caress the slumbering ground,
Each pause a blessing, a sacred sound.
The horizon painted in soft pastels,
A canvas of dreams where wonder dwells.

Beneath the white, life stirs and awakes,
In the quietude, every heart aches.
For the cycle continues, as seasons will shift,
When nature takes pause, we embrace the gift.

Eyes close softly to absorb every hue,
Building a wonderland, fresh and anew.
In the stillness, find joy in each breath,
As nature unfolds her beauty and depth.

Quietude in White

A blanket of snow, soft and light,
Whispers of calm in the quiet night.
Footsteps muffled, the world at peace,
In the stillness, all worries cease.

Branches glisten, frost on display,
Nature's art in a pure ballet.
Stars peer down through the crystal air,
In this serene moment, none can compare.

Breathe in the silence, inhale the grace,
Wrapped in the warmth of winter's embrace.
Each flake a promise of dreams untold,
In quietude's arms, we're gently enfolded.

A soft glow rises, dawn's gentle kiss,
Snowflakes dance in a world full of bliss.
Heartbeats sync with the rhythm of white,
In the purity, everything feels right.

A Lullaby of Ice

Under the moon's sleepy silver gaze,
Icicles shimmer in wintry haze.
The world draped in a crystalline sheet,
A soft lullaby, hushed and sweet.

Snowflakes whisper their gentle song,
A symphony where the cold belongs.
Like lullabies sung through the silent night,
Wrapping dreams in its frosty light.

Each glistening surface reflects the stars,
A magic hidden in ice's bars.
Close your eyes to the dance of the chill,
Let the frost cradle you, soft and still.

In the stillness, time seems to freeze,
A moment of wonder on a gentle breeze.
Nature's soft breath on a cold winter's eve,
In the lullaby of ice, we quietly believe.

As dawn breaks softly, the world awakens,
With warmth and light, all worries shaken.
Yet in our hearts, a chill remains,
The echoes of ice in our refrains.

The Calm Before the Storm

Nature holds its breath, a pause so deep,
The air electric, excitement we keep.
Clouds gather round, a heavy veil,
In the hush, whispers dance on the gale.

Birds take flight, swift in their quest,
Seeking shelter, a cozy nest.
Leaves sway gently, a precursor's sigh,
The calm wraps all as the winds start to cry.

Anticipation hangs thick in the air,
The world awaits with a heightened stare.
A deep rumble echoes, the sky's display,
In this stillness, we know change is on the way.

With each passing moment, tension shall rise,
Thunder rolls softly beneath cloudy skies.
Like a heartbeat, the storm draws near,
In this calm, we feel both hope and fear.

The first raindrop falls, breaking the trance,
A wild symphony begins to dance.
Yet in the quiet, we felt it grow,
A reminder that life is a dynamic flow.

Frost-Kissed Solitude

In a world of frost, I find my peace,
Wrapped in nature's tender release.
The silence breaks, a gentle sigh,
With every breath, I feel the sky.

Footprints trailing through crisp, pure snow,
A path of solitude, where whispers flow.
Each crystal flake tells a tale of old,
In this winter's embrace, I'm quietly bold.

The trees stand tall, adorned in white,
Guardians of silence, soft in the light.
A refuge found where the chill meets heart,
In frost-kissed moments, I find my start.

With every gust, the world seems to pause,
In the cold, I find warmth, a hidden cause.
Beneath the surface, life's beauty will bloom,
In solitude's arms, I find space to loom.

So here I linger, lost in the calm,
Embracing the winter, like an old psalm.
In the frost's delicate hold, I unfold,
A tapestry woven with threads of gold.

Serene Blanket of White

The snow falls softly, a gentle sigh,
Covering the earth, a lullaby.
Each flake a whisper, a dream taking flight,
In this quiet moment, all feels right.

A world transformed, in silence it basks,
Nature's pure canvas, no questions, no tasks.
Frosted branches, each tree a gem,
Beneath this blanket, peace flows like a hem.

Footprints are hidden, paths fade away,
Lost in the beauty of this winter day.
The sun peeks through, a soft golden glow,
Illuminates wonders, the world laid low.

Children are laughing, their joy takes flight,
Building snowmen, hearts warm with delight.
In a serene moment, we all can find,
Happiness blooms, leaving cares behind.

Muffled Footsteps in the Cold

In the hush of twilight, footsteps grow near,
Crunching on snow, crisp and clear.
Each step tells a tale, a story untold,
Muffled and gentle, in the bitter cold.

A breath escapes, a puff of white,
Painting the air in the fading light.
The world is a canvas, untouched and pure,
A sanctuary found, a heart can endure.

The trees stand watch, in their icy embrace,
Guardians of secrets, a mystical space.
Whispers of winter weave through the night,
Inviting the stars, in their shimmering light.

Shadows grow long, as the daylight roams,
Muffled footsteps lead us back home.
With each careful step, we leave our fears,
In the depth of the night, find peace in our tears.

Solitude in a Snowbound World

In a snowbound world, tranquility reigns,
Amidst the silence, the heart breaks chains.
Loneliness whispers in the shimmering cold,
A solace discovered, stories unfold.

The wind has a song, a gentle refrain,
Dancing through branches, freeing the pain.
Each flake is a promise, a moment to hold,
In solitude's comfort, we find warmth bold.

Frozen lakes glisten, reflections so bright,
Mirroring dreams in the pale moonlight.
With every glance, wonders appear,
In a snowbound world, we let go of fear.

Beneath the vast sky, we wander and roam,
Finding connections in this frozen home.
Nature enfolds us, heart to heart,
In its pure embrace, we learn to restart.

The Stillness of Icebound Trees

Icebound trees stand with elegance rare,
Draped in crystals, a breathtaking layer.
Their branches like fingers, reaching for stars,
Guardians of secrets, healers of scars.

Silence hangs heavy, the world holds its breath,
In this winter wonder, a moment of rest.
Each twig is adorned, a delicate lace,
A tribute to time, a frozen embrace.

The stillness enchants, paints shadows on white,
Nature's quiet song, a melody light.
In the hush of their strength, the stories they keep,
Whisper of winters, of seasons asleep.

With the breath of the wind, they sway to and fro,
Telling the tales only they truly know.
Among icebound sentinels, serenity lies,
In the stillness of trees, the heart learns to rise.

Soft Footfalls on Frozen Ground

In the twilight's gentle glow,
Footsteps whisper, soft and low.
Crunch of frost beneath my stride,
Nature's hush, a tranquil guide.

Trees stand tall in silent grace,
Blanketed in winter's lace.
Every branch, a crystal hue,
The world awakens, fresh and new.

Crisp air dances with delight,
Stars emerge, a sparkling sight.
Moonlight paints the earth in white,
Soft footfalls in the night.

A moment held, so pure, so bright,
Frozen ground beneath my light.
In this stillness, peace does bloom,
Easing hearts, dispelling gloom.

Life's rhythm slows, the world at rest,
In the quiet, we are blessed.
Soft footfalls on this frozen ground,
In nature's arms, our solace found.

Silence of Hidden Pond

Beneath the trees, a stillness lies,
Rippling gently, where water sighs.
Reflections dance on glassy sheen,
Secrets shared, yet seldom seen.

Frogs croak soft, the night draws near,
In this place, there's only cheer.
Moonbeams touch the surface light,
As whispers fade into the night.

Dragonflies flit on gossamer wings,
Nature's peace, oh, how it sings.
In the silence, life unfolds,
Stories whispered, quiet, bold.

Leaves rustle like a distant song,
In this haven, we belong.
Calm descends, a soothing balm,
Here, our hearts forever calm.

The hidden pond, a sacred space,
Where time stands still, and dreams embrace.
In gentle silence, souls can mend,
Where nature's grace will never end.

Dreaming in Frosted Shadows

Underneath the silver glow,
Frosted shadows start to flow.
Dreams entwined in winter's kiss,
Moments frozen, pure bliss.

Moonlit fields clad in white,
Crisp and clear, a magic sight.
Footsteps trace a path unknown,
In the stillness, seeds are sown.

Whispers echo through the pines,
Stories told by ancient lines.
Nature holds her breath in peace,
In this realm, our worries cease.

Time drips slowly, like the snow,
Enchanting all it meets below.
Dreaming in these frosted hues,
Wrapped in quiet, we renew.

Every flake, a fleeting dream,
Illuminated by moonbeam.
Frosted shadows softly play,
Guiding hearts till break of day.

The Breath of Cold Mornings

As dawn breaks in a chilly haze,
Nature stirs in morning's gaze.
Puffs of breath like clouds do rise,
Painting warmth in winter skies.

Frosted grass beneath my feet,
Crunching softly, crisp and sweet.
Birds take flight, a morning song,
Welcoming the light so strong.

The world awakens, shades of gold,
In this moment, life unfolds.
Cold whispers dance on gentle air,
A symphony of joy laid bare.

Steam from tea warms up my hands,
In this stillness, peace expands.
The breath of mornings, cold yet bright,
Filling hearts with pure delight.

Foggy fields like dreams arise,
In the chill, the spirit flies.
A day begins, a canvas wide,
With the breath of cold as guide.

Melodies of Muffled Night

Whispers dance in shadows deep,
While the world lies fast asleep.
Stars twinkle in silent grace,
As dreams drift in soft embrace.

Stillness reigns, a soothing balm,
Wrapped in night, the air is calm.
Crickets sing their lullabies,
Underneath the velvet skies.

Ticking clocks mark quiet time,
In this world, all thoughts sublime.
Moonlight paints with silver hue,
Every spark of night feels new.

Branches sway, a gentle sway,
In the hush of fading day.
Nature hums a secret tune,
Echoing beneath the moon.

In the dark, our fears take flight,
Melodies of muffled night.
Awake within our hearts they dwell,
In silence, we have much to tell.

Clouds of Stillness

Pillow clouds drift slow and wide,
In the sky, a tranquil tide.
Gentle whispers, soft and clear,
Nature's voice for all to hear.

Sunlight breaks, a golden stream,
Painting shadows, brightening dreams.
Birds take flight in graceful arcs,
Chasing daylight, leaving marks.

Beneath the heavens' blue expanse,
Silent moments sway and dance.
Peaceful sighs fill open air,
As hearts release their every care.

Each soft breeze, a tender sigh,
Caressing earth as it passes by.
In the stillness, a lover's vow,
Promises made in the here and now.

Clouds of white, a calming sight,
Woven dreams in day and night.
In this hush, our souls align,
Finding solace, pure and divine.

The Blanketed Earth

Blanketed in winter's grace,
Nature wears a frosty face.
Silent fields, a sight serene,
Purest white, a gentle sheen.

Trees adorned in crystal lace,
Crisp and quiet, holding space.
Footsteps crunch on frozen ground,
In this hush, new life is found.

Snowflakes fall like whispered dreams,
Shimmering with silver beams.
Beauty lies in every flake,
In this peace, the world awakes.

Underneath this frosty cover,
Nature sleeps, as if to hover.
Time stands still, a moment bright,
Wrapped in warmth on winter's night.

The blanketed earth, so pure,
Holds a promise, soft and sure.
In its depths, the warmth resides,
Awaiting spring's embrace and tides.

Underneath the Shroud of Ice

Underneath the shroud of ice,
Lies a world, so cold and nice.
Frozen lakes and crystal streams,
Whisper secrets in our dreams.

Branches heavy with glistening weight,
Cloaked in winter, watching fate.
Silence shrouds the waking land,
Nature pauses, still and grand.

Echoes of a distant past,
Memories that hold us fast.
In this chill, a heart can yearn,
For the warmth that spring will churn.

Every flake, a story told,
In the frost, a whisper bold.
Underneath the winter's guise,
Hope and life shall rise and rise.

As the thaw begins to hum,
Life returns, the birds will come.
But until then, we watch and wait,
Underneath the shroud, so great.

Shiver of Shadows

Whispers dance as moonlight glows,
Shadows stretch where calm wind blows.
Figures flicker, forms that hide,
Veils of darkness, secrets abide.

Branches creak in eerie tune,
Nighttime blooms beneath the moon.
A chill seeps through the silent trees,
Echoing softly in the breeze.

Eyes that glimmer, watchful stare,
Curtains drawn with careful care.
Footsteps falter, hearts will race,
Lost in that haunting, ancient space.

Fear intertwines with night's embrace,
In shadows' depths, none dare to trace.
A world unseen, yet deeply felt,
Where tales of old in silence dwelt.

The dawn will chase these phantoms away,
Yet in their wake, they gently sway.
A shiver lingers, memories cast,
In whispers of shadows that forever last.

Soft Footfalls on Frost

In the hush of early dawn,
Footsteps light on frozen lawn.
Crystals sparkle in soft light,
Nature stretches, calm and bright.

Breath like smoke in the still air,
Every movement, slow and rare.
Winter's cloak, a gentle sheet,
Treads softly, where all is sweet.

Birds do sing, though shadows creep,
In the quiet, secrets keep.
Over fields where silence falls,
Echoes dance from wooden walls.

Each step whispers of the cold,
Tales of winter, softly told.
Nature's canvas, pure and white,
Paints a scene of pure delight.

As the sun begins to rise,
Colors bloom, surprising eyes.
Soft footfalls in this wonder,
Mingle with the morning thunder.

Hibernation's Embrace

Nestled deep in winter's fold,
Creatures rest, the air turns cold.
Dreams of spring in silence play,
Nature pauses, lost in gray.

Beneath the snow, life takes a breath,
Wrapped in warmth, defying death.
Faint thumps echo in the night,
Hope stirs gently, holding tight.

In burrows deep, the stillness hums,
Waiting for the thawing drums.
The world outside wears icy skin,
While within, there's warmth akin.

Softly tucked in wool and leaf,
Time stands still, a soft motif.
Nature sleeps, yet dreams anew,
In time, blossoms will break through.

Hibernation cradles all,
In its arms, so warm and small.
Embrace this time, for seasons change,
Life will bloom, and hearts rearrange.

A Palette of Chill

Brush of frost on morning glass,
Colors fade as hours pass.
Windswept hues, a muted show,
Canvas dressed in winter's glow.

Blue and gray in soft cascade,
Nature's art, a lovely shade.
Pale horizons, whisper low,
Each stroke speaks of ice and snow.

Crimson leaves in memory kept,
Under blankets where dreams slept.
Nature's palette, cold and bright,
Colors dance in fading light.

The chill wraps 'round like gentle hands,
Filling spaces, where warmth stands.
With every breath, a story spun,
In colors of the winter sun.

A tapestry of cold embrace,
In every corner, every space.
Though chill may reign, there lies a thrill,
In every shade of winter's chill.

The Poetry of Stillness

In quiet corners, shadows lay,
The world holds breaths, it finds its way.
Soft whispers dance in muted air,
A moment's pause, a silent prayer.

The trees stand tall, their secrets tight,
The moon spills silver, gentle light.
Time drifts softly, hearts align,
In every heartbeat, peace we find.

Stars blink slowly, tales untold,
Wrapped in dreams, we watch unfold.
In stillness, echoes softly sing,
A symphony of everything.

Beneath the surface, calm abides,
A tranquil sea where stillness hides.
With every breath, we draw it near,
The poetry of silence clear.

Embrace the quiet, let it lead,
In stillness, heart and soul take heed.
Through whispered dreams, we journey on,
In the poetry of silent dawn.

Barren Beauty

In empty fields where shadows play,
The barren earth takes center stage.
With faded hues and lines so stark,
Life whispers softly, leaving marks.

The skeletal trees reach for the sky,
In their stillness, secrets lie.
A rugged path through dust and stone,
In barren beauty, stillness grown.

Windswept landscapes, a haunting song,
A testament where dreams belong.
In silence, nature's grace extended,
In barren lands, life is suspended.

Fractured light on weathered ground,
In desolation, beauty found.
Each cracked surface tells a tale,
Of strength and hope when all seems pale.

The barren beauty, fierce and cruel,
Reflects the heart, a hidden jewel.
Through lifeless veins, the spirit weaves,
In empty spaces, life believes.

A rise, a fall, the cycle's plight,
In barren beauty, shines the light.
From desolate scenes, strength appears,
Where beauty dwells, facing fears.

Frozen Whispers

In winter's grip, the world asleep,
The air is thick, the silence deep.
Each breath a cloud, each step a sound,
In frozen whispers, peace is found.

The trees adorned in crystal lace,
A stunning scene, a quiet grace.
With every flake that softly falls,
A hush descends, nature calls.

Underneath the frost, life waits,
In hidden depths, it contemplates.
With stillness wrapped in winter's cloak,
Each frozen whisper softly spoke.

Through icy paths, reflections bright,
The world transformed by shimmering light.
In quiet moments, hearts connect,
In frozen whispers, we reflect.

A symphony of crisp, cold air,
In every heartbeat, winter's care.
As shadows linger, spirits rise,
In frozen whispers, hope defies.

With dawn's first glow, the silence breaks,
In every shimmer, wonder wakes.
A world reborn, alive with sound,
In frozen whispers, joy is found.

Asleep Beneath the Stars

The night extends a velvet hand,
As dreams take flight across the land.
With twinkling lights in skies so vast,
We drift away, the moments past.

Beneath the stars, the world retreats,
In quiet hum, the heartbeat beats.
Each twinkle tells a story bright,
Of love and dreams that fill the night.

The moon it smiles, a guardian near,
In shadows cast, we hold what's dear.
With every sigh, the worries cease,
Asleep beneath the stars, we find peace.

A cosmic dance, the universe spins,
In whispered dreams, the sun begins.
With every glance, we see the grace,
Of gentle night, a warm embrace.

The quiet rustle of the leaves,
Carries the dreams the night conceives.
With every star, a wish we send,
Asleep beneath the stars, we mend.

In twilight's glow, the heart takes flight,
In slumber's arms, all is right.
Under a canopy of light,
Asleep beneath the stars tonight.

Milton Keynes UK
Ingram Content Group UK Ltd.
UKHW021045031224
452078UK00010B/596